*T*here is no friendship, no love,
like that of the parent for the child.

🖐🖐 *Henry Ward Beecher*

Blue Mountain Arts®

Other books in the *Shapes of Life*™ series...

Believe & Succeed

Daughters

Friendship

Girlfriends

Great Teachers

Love

Marriage

Mothers

Sisters

Sons

Words for Teenagers

A Blue Mountain Arts® Collection
on What It Means
to Be a Parent

Edited by Patricia Wayant

Blue Mountain Press™

Boulder, Colorado

Copyright © 2004 by Blue Mountain Arts, Inc.

All rights reserved. No part of this publication may be reproduced, stored in a retrieval system, or transmitted in any form or by any means, electronic, mechanical, photocopying, recording or otherwise, without the written permission of the publisher.

We wish to thank Susan Polis Schutz for permission to reprint the following poems that appear in this publication: "When you interact with your children..." and "Children Are Love." Copyright © 1984, 1988 by Stephen Schutz and Susan Polis Schutz. All rights reserved.

Library of Congress Control Number: 2004108461
ISBN: 0-88396-879-7

ACKNOWLEDGMENTS appear at end of book.

Certain trademarks are used under license.
BLUE MOUNTAIN PRESS is registered in U.S. Patent and Trademark Office.

Manufactured in Thailand.
First Printing: 2004

 This book is printed on recycled paper.

Blue Mountain Arts, Inc.

P.O. Box 4549, Boulder, Colorado 80306

Contents

(Authors listed in order of first appearance)

Children Are Life's Greatest Gift

From baby, to child, to young adult, they are full of life and filled with surprises. In every one of their years, they give you more happiness and love than most people will ever dream of.

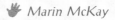 *Marin McKay*

Being a parent means that you have the opportunity to experience loving someone more than you love yourself. It's learning what it's like to experience joy and pain through someone else's life.

— *Barbara Cage*

*I*n your children's happiest and most exciting moments, your heart will celebrate and smile beside them.

In their lowest lows, your love will be there to keep them warm, to give them strength, and to remind them that the sunshine is sure to come again.

In their moments of accomplishment, you will be filled so full of pride that you may have a hard time keeping the feeling inside you.

In their moments of disappointment, you will be a shoulder to cry on, a hand to hold, and a love that will gently enfold them until everything's okay.

In their gray days, you will help them search, one by one, for the colors of the rainbow.

In their bright and shining hours, you will be smiling, too, right along beside them.

Throughout their life, you will love them and care for them.

— Laurel Atherton

I thought I knew what love
*   was all about*
until the day my child was born.
Suddenly, I felt an instant swell
of pride and joy within my heart.
My thoughts were overwhelmed
*   with fierce protection,*
future plans and hopes,
and dreams for my child's happiness.

Barbara J. Hall

When your children are very, very
small, you dance with them cradled
in your arms.
They are precious angels,
and when you hold them close,
love overwhelms you.

You wonder what kind of life
   they will lead.
What will be their first word,
   their first job?
What kind of person will they become?
And will their life take them
   far away from you?

Then you hold them even closer.
You give them an extra kiss
and an extra squeeze,
and whisper "I love you" one more time.
You know they are too young to remember
   your words,
but you hope they will never forget them.

❦ ❦ Kathryn Higginbottom Gorin

*The decision to have a child
is momentous. It is to decide
forever after to have your
heart go walking around
outside your body.*

Elizabeth Stone

Children Are Love,

Children have a
fondness for everything
Their absolute sweetness is enveloped
   in a beautiful innocence

Children have an
unbridled enthusiasm and
a willingness to share everything they have
Their absolute goodness is shrouded by a
complete gentleness and sensitivity

An aura of
peace
truth and
wonder
radiates from children
They are angels of
kindness
sweetness
caring and
love

Susan Polis Schutz

A child is a wonderful blessing
that opens up a whole new world
  for you.
Never again will you love anything
  or anyone in quite the same way,
or be as protective, devoted, or giving.

                    ❦❦ Barbara Cage

C hild of mine, what you are
is everything that means
anything to me. You are the most
perfect moments of my entire life:
moments of memories and sweet,
precious times. You are sunlight that
shines on the world and goodness
that contains all the hopes of my
universe. You are eyes that lovingly
encourage me to see things the way
you do, and I will always be grateful
for the chance to share that view.
You are the miracle of a million
things, all wrapped up in the present
of one incredibly special person. You
are a gift unlike any other; a treasure
beyond the measure of any possible
value; and an inspiration that
surpasses the creation of every
masterpiece, imagined or real.

Child of mine, you are the most
wonderful joy there will ever be.
And you are so dearly loved... by me.

🖐 Laurel Atherton

What Makes a Good Parent?

Good parents know what it means to love... to show their child right from wrong and to instill decent values... to give their child a wonderful childhood full of precious memories.

🖐 *T. L. Nash*

*T*o raise a child to be a person of worth requires a parent's caring use of so many special talents...

It requires someone who understands that a child has feelings that change from day to day, and each feeling needs love and nurturing.

It requires someone to receive those feelings as they would their own — handling each with honesty, gentleness, and care.

It takes a heart above the rest of the world to see a child's potential, to draw it out, to encourage their dreams, and to help with their plans.

To raise a child to be a person of worth takes someone who can give that child so many reasons to believe they're a special someone on this earth.

 Barbara J. Hall

The Definition of a Good Father

He believes in the family and in keeping it strong, close, and loving.

He defines his role in life by upholding the best traditions of fatherhood and transforming the rest in order to meet the demands of a constantly changing world.

A father welcomes and enjoys the commitment of time and effort that a family represents. He knows that it is important to show all his emotions — fear and sadness as well as strength and happiness.

He is committed to a set of values, yet he is also open to changing those beliefs when confronting new situations.

He strives quietly and often without thanks to make this world a better place for all future generations.

🌿 Edmund O'Neill

The Definition of a Good Mother

She is a teacher — helping her children to learn about life, pointing them in the right direction, letting them make their own mistakes and then helping them pick up the pieces afterwards.

She is a friend — listening to her children when they need to talk, making them talk when they don't know they need to, supporting them when they are down, and helping them to see that things aren't all that bad.

She is a role model — leading her children by example. But most of all, she loves unconditionally no matter what her children do or say, letting them know that they are not alone and never will be, for they will always have a home.

🌿 Deborah A. Brideau

In my dealing with my child, my Latin and Greek, my accomplishments and my money stead me nothing, but as much soul as I have avails.

🖐 Ralph Waldo Emerson

When you interact with your children
you must always keep in mind
that everything you do and say to them
has an enormous impact on their lives
If you treat your children
with love and respect
they will love and respect themselves
    and others
If you treat your children
    with intelligence and honesty
they will develop confidence in their
    abilities to make decisions
If you treat your children with happiness
    and gentleness
they will develop into happy, stable adults
who will be capable of enjoying life

— Susan Polis Schutz

The greatest parents are those who raise their children in an environment of caring, encouragement, and love. Their influence on their children's lives is woven into the stories they tell, the hugs they give, the tears they dry, the laughter they inspire, and the wisdom they share.

🌿 R. L. Keith

A Parent's Creed

As a parent, I will
set an example for my child
by being positive and showing compassion
   for those less fortunate.
I will take time to listen —
understanding a child's need
to share a problem or success with someone.
I will remember to thank my child
for being an important part of my life.
I will make every effort each day
to read with my child and help establish
a genuine love of books.
I will show kindness to all living creatures,
so my child may better understand
   the value of life.
I will explore nature with my child
as we observe the first signs of spring,
the color of autumn leaves,
the beauty of a snowflake,
and the orange glow of a winter sunset.
Every day, through my example,
my child will know how much I really care.

❧ Rogene N. Penny

You Will Learn and Grow Together

Just as parents help shape children, children help shape parents.

🤚🤚 *Marian Wright Edelman*

When my child came into this world and into my life, so many beautiful things happened. Although I was the one holding him, he was the one enfolding so many of my hopes and dreams. Although I was the one who was supposed to teach him all the things to do as he grew up, he was the one who taught me — constantly — of my capacity to love, to experience life in its most meaningful way, and to open my heart wide enough to let all those joyful feelings inside.

Laurel Atherton

With exquisite joy and delight, I have watched my daughter grow and marveled at the mysteries and curiosities of each stage unraveling before my eyes... She has enriched my life more than she'll ever know, and she has taught me so much about being a parent, a mom, a friend... and a person.

Debbie Burton-Peddle

Children help us
to experience again...

*T*he joy and enthusiasm of looking forward
to each new day with glorious
expectations of wonderful things to come;
The vision that sees the world as a splendid
place with good fairies, brave knights, and
glistening castles reaching toward the sky;
The radiant curiosity that finds adventure in
simple things: the mystery of billowy
clouds, the miracle of snowflakes, the
magic of growing flowers;
The tolerance that forgets differences as quickly
as your childish quarrels are spent, that
holds no grudges, that hates never, that
loves people for what they are;
The genuineness of being oneself; to be done
with sham, pretense, and empty show; to
be simple, natural, and sincere;
The courage that rises from defeat and tries
again, as the child with laughing face
rebuilds the house of blocks that topples to
the floor;
The contented, trusting mind that, at the close of
day, woos the blessing of child-like slumber.

🌺 Author Unknown

*P*arenting forces us to get to know ourselves better than we ever might have imagined we could — and in many new ways.... We'll discover talents we never dreamed we had and fervently wish for others at moments we feel we desperately need them. As time goes on, we'll probably discover that we have more to give and can give more than we ever imagined.

🖐🖐 *Fred Rogers*

*T*here will be moments when all you'll want to do is hold your child in your arms and tell him everything will be all right. But, as a parent, sometimes your job will be more than just giving a reassuring hug. You will have to let him find out things for himself, even when the outcome is painful. It won't be easy, but if you allow him to think that any problem he ever has will go away just by wishful thinking, you won't be fulfilling your role as a parent.

Children have to learn and grow through their own trials and experiences. By encouraging them to be themselves, to feel comfortable with who they are, and not to let any obstacle in front of them frighten them away, slowly but surely they will build self-confidence and courage.

🌱 T. L. Nash

Love Is the Greatest Gift You Can Give Your Children

The greatest happiness of life is the conviction that we are loved.

🖐🖐 *Victor Hugo*

Once you have a child, everything that existed before is different, new, and exciting. Your life changes in a way that you couldn't imagine before. You look at your child and realize that you are a different person now. Perspectives have changed. Priorities have switched. Your eyes are opened to see the world in a new and different light.

Yes, there are worries and concerns, responsibilities and obligations, but these are taken in stride — one at a time. The best that you can give your child is the beautiful simplicity of your love, each and every day. A child who knows such love is a child who possesses riches beyond measure.

🖐 Debbie Burton-Peddle

More than money or items of material worth, children will remember the moments you were there when they needed you, the kisses you showered on them, the big bear hugs where you both ended up laughing on the floor, the cup of hot cocoa you made when they were sick, and, yes, even the time you shouted "I love you" in front of all their friends.

Anna Marie Edwards

unlike most careers, parenthood is one full of emotional ups and downs. No one is more important than those you are in charge of. Every mistake, slip-up, or decision can have you wondering and second-guessing yourself, your motives, and your expertise. You may long for peace and instead get pouting and rebellion.

When difficult times seem overwhelming and you wonder whatever possessed you to become a parent in the first place, remember... the answer is love.

It's love that will see you through every heartache and worry. Love will soothe, kiss, and hug away fears and sadness. It's love that is balanced with discipline and caring, humor and responsibility, love that can say no when it's the best answer and yes whenever possible. This kind of love never disappears, even when everything else seems to — because the love of a parent is the only kind guaranteed to be unconditional and never-ending.

🌿 Barbara Cage

What comes from the heart,
goes to the heart.

✋ *Samuel Taylor Coleridge*

If there could be only one thing in life to teach your children, teach them to love...
To respect others so that they may find respect in themselves;
To learn the value of giving, so that if ever there comes a time in their lives when someone is really in need, they will give;
To act in a manner that they would wish to be treated; to be proud of themselves;
To laugh and smile as much as they can, in order to help bring joy back into this world;
To have faith in others; to be understanding;
To stand tall in this world and to learn to depend on themselves;
To only take from this earth those things which they really need, so there will be enough for others;
To not depend on money or material things for their happiness, but
To learn to appreciate the people who love them and to find peace and security within themselves...
For all these things are love.

— Donna Dargis

Letting Go Is the Hardest Part of All

*There are two lasting bequests we can hope to give our children.
One of these is roots; the other, wings.*

🖐 *Hodding Carter*

A child enters your home and for the next twenty years makes so much noise you can hardly stand it. The child departs, leaving the house so silent you think you are going mad.

🖐 John Andrew Holmes

*I*f we [are] successful in teaching independent decision making and engendering the trust of our children, then we can say we have achieved a great goal: teaching our children to get along without parents. And as most parents quickly learn, being rid of their parents is also the goal of most children!

🖐 Bob Keeshan (Captain Kangaroo)

Children are our future
Their tiny footsteps
grow into our shoes.
Their delicate smiles
are our future happiness.
Their courage
is our future strength.
Their thoughtfulness
is our future community.
Their wisdom
is our future wealth.
Children are our future.
Let our future shine!

 Lisa Marie Brennan

Watching my son grow up has been the greatest experience of my life, but it's gone by so fast. It seems like yesterday he was toddling his first steps. I can still see him chasing butterflies, riding his tricycle, hitting his first home run, fishing at the river, and all the millions of details from his boyhood now left behind.

He has taught me more about life and love than I could ever teach him. Letting him go a little at a time has been my greatest challenge and effort in life. The tiny baby, the child with a thousand questions, the curious adolescent, and the interesting teen still live in my heart as I see him now — the young man he has become.

And I am still in awe when I reach up and wrap my arms around his broad shoulders in my attempt to still hold him in my arms.

❦ Sylvia Kurath

Being a parent has given me happiness to the greatest degree and warmth that fills my heart. I am in awe that my child came into my life and made my dreams come true.

Barbara Cage

From the moment my daughter was born, she became the focal point of my existence. Her smile was the sunshine in my heart. Her happiness was the only treasure I sought.

And so began the great paradox of parenthood. For when her tiny hand touched mine, I knew that I had been chosen to nurture her, love her, and then give her the strength to let go.

Letting go is not easy. But I look at her now — a beautiful young woman, strong in her convictions and determined to face life on her own terms — and I still feel my heart swell with pride and joy.

My dreams for her life might not always be the same ones she seeks. But one thing remains the same: her happiness will always be my greatest treasure. I know now that the true miracle of that first touch lies in one simple truth: even though her hand may slip away from mine, we will hold each other in our hearts forever.

Nancy Gilliam

*P*arents' hearts are always
with their children.

🖐 *Anonymous*

*T*hey're our babies in blankets, nurtured, loved, and cuddled. People tell us to cherish this time because it goes by too quickly. Then one day we understand the truth of those words — when our children have grown from all those precious first moments that turned into days, months, and then years.

Suddenly our children are standing in front of us as the young adults they've become. They talk of cars, college, apartments, and places that are just too far from home. We cry sometimes from knowing that soon they will wake up in a different place and leave wet towels on the floor of their own bathroom. We would give anything to have them home again to tell them to clean up their room, pick up their stuff, and stop fighting.

From our hearts they were conceived, raised, and guided one little foot in front of the other. They will leave home, but no matter where life takes them, they will never leave that place in our hearts. In that place, those babies in blankets — the memories and moments — are with us every day, and they are ours to love forever.

🖐 Cindy VanDenBosch

Time will pass by,
and so many things will change,
but the absolute joy
a child brings to life
will only grow deeper
and more important.

Deanna Beisser

As a parent, you want to be a place your children can come to... for shelter, for unconditional caring, for sharing all the support one person can give. You want to be a person they can turn to... for answers and understanding, or just to reinforce the feeling of how incredibly special they are.

You want to do everything you possibly can for them because that's what love does when it is strong and grateful and giving. You want them to know what a gift it is to be their parent and that your love for them is never-ending.

— Douglas Pagels

The Bond Between Parent and Child Lasts a Lifetime

The bond between parent and child
is a special one.
It remains unchanged by time or distance.
It is the purest love —
unconditional and true.
It is understanding of any situation
and forgiving of any mistake.
It creates a support that is constant
while everything else changes.
It is a friendship based on mutual love,
respect, and a genuine liking
of each other as a person.
It is knowing that no matter
where you go or who you are,
there is someone who truly loves you
and is always there to support and console you.
When a situation seems impossible
you make it through together
by holding on to each other.

The bond between parent and child
is strong enough to withstand
harsh words and hurt feelings,
for it is smart enough to always
see the love beyond the words.
It is brave enough to always speak the truth,
even when lies would be easier.
It is always there —
    anytime, anywhere —
whenever it is needed.
It is a gift held in the heart and in the soul,
and it cannot be taken away
or exchanged for another.
To possess this love is a treasure
that makes life more valuable.

— Stephanie Douglass

ACKNOWLEDGMENTS

We gratefully acknowledge the permission granted by the following authors, publishers, and authors' representatives to reprint poems or excerpts from their publications.

Elizabeth Stone for "The decision to have a child...." Copyright © by Elizabeth Stone. All rights reserved.

Barbara J. Hall for "To raise a child to be person of worth...." Copyright © 2004 by Barbara J. Hall. All rights reserved.

Rogene N. Penny for "A Parent's Creed." Copyright © 2004 by Rogene N. Penny. All rights reserved.

Beacon Press for "Just as parents help shape children..." from THE MEASURE OF OUR SUCCESS by Marian Wright Edelman. Copyright © 1992 by Marian Wright Edelman. All rights reserved.

Berkley Publishing Group, a division of Penguin Group (USA) Inc., for "Parenting forces us to get to know ourselves..." from MISTER ROGERS TALKS WITH PARENTS by Fred Rogers. Copyright © 1986 by Fred Rogers. All rights reserved.

Debbie Burton-Peddle for "Once you have a child...." Copyright © 2004 by Debbie Burton-Peddle. All rights reserved.

Doubleday, a division of Random House, Inc., for "If we [are] successful in teaching..." from GROWING UP HAPPY by Bob Keeshan. Copyright © 1989 by Bob Keeshan. All rights reserved.

Lisa Marie Brennan for "Children are our future...." Copyright © 2004 by Lisa Marie Brennan. All rights reserved.

Sylvia Kurath for "Watching my son grow up...." Copyright © 2004 by Sylvia Kurath. All rights reserved.

Cindy VanDenBosch for "They're our babies in blankets...." Copyright © 2004 by Cindy VanDenBosch. All rights reserved.

A careful effort has been made to trace the ownership of selections used in this anthology in order to obtain permission to reprint copyrighted material and give proper credit to the copyright owners. If any error or omission has occurred, it is completely inadvertent, and we would like to make corrections in future editions provided that written notification is made to the publisher:

BLUE MOUNTAIN ARTS, INC., P.O. Box 4549, Boulder, Colorado 80306.